Together In Peace And Harmony, Book 1

PRESCHOOL FRIENDS

A-Z

AROUND THE WORLD

WRITTEN BY FLO BARNETT

ILLUSTRATED BY JAMES AMBROUS

PRESCHOOL FRIENDS A-Z AROUND THE WORLD
Copyright © 2016 by Flo Barnett
All rights reserved. No part of this book may be used or reproduced in
any manner whatsoever without written permission except in the case of brief
quotations embodied in critical articles and reviews.

Illustrated by James Ambrous

For my highly determined grandson, Gabe,
and for all the children of the world,

Embrace diversity and live together in peace and harmony.

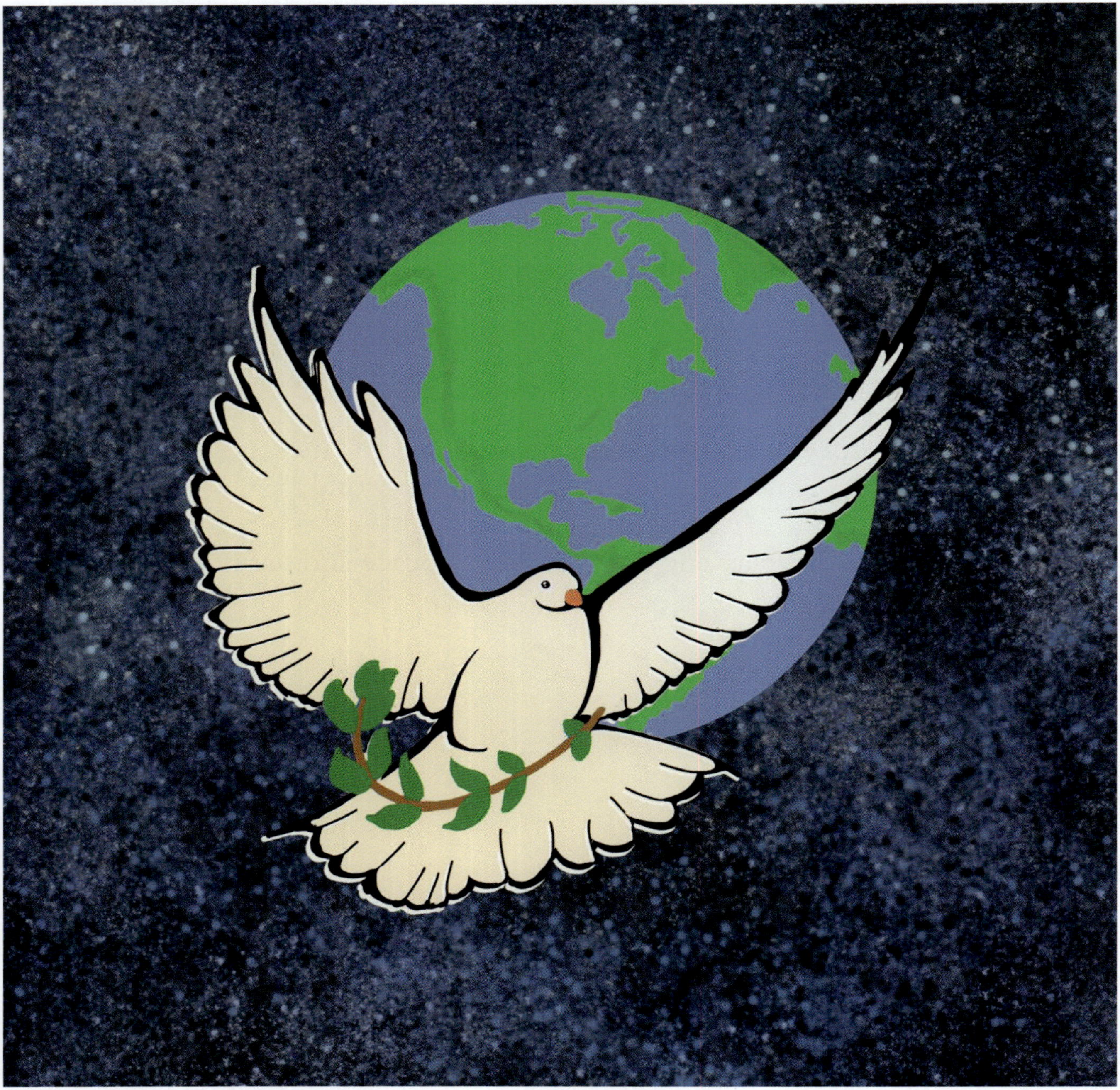

PRESCHOOL FRIENDS
Have different names,
Quite special from A to Z.
They've come from all around the world
Just to play with you and me!

A

ARKA
(Turkish – friend)
Waves as friends come in
Skipping through the classroom door.
"Want to play a game with me?
Come, sit right here on the floor."

BAO
(Vietnamese – protector)
Hunts fierce lions,
In dark camouflage he's dressed.
Protecting all from danger,
With courage he faces the test

CARINA
(Italian – little darling)
Hugs her dolly
While singing a lullaby.
"Sleep well, my little darling,
Hush now, please don't you cry.

DAVID
(Scottish - beloved)
Is loved by everyone,
Always glad to answer his call,
Happy to follow behind him
As he scales the climbing wall.

ELISE
(French – loyal one)
Is loyal to all,
Her promises so sincere.
She'll safely guard your secrets.
You can whisper them in her ear.

FIALA
(Czech – violet flower)
Peeks out shyly
Like a violet in the snow.
A friend sits close beside her,
Smiling and saying, "hello."

GAMILA
(Egyptian – beauty)
A real beauty,
Loves to play dress-up you see,
A gown and a crown for her,
An eyepatch and sword for me.

HASAN
(Swahili – handsome)
Is very handsome,
Bright eyes, brown skin, and a smile.
We put on suits and big ties,
And play 'Daddy's Work' for a while.

I

IOLANI
(Hawaiian – soars like a hawk)
Soars upward
Like a mighty hawk in the sky,
As she swings in the sunshine,
Pretending that she can fly!

JU-LONG
(Chinese – powerful dragon)
Roams the playground,
A powerful dragon of yore.
Stretching his arms to catch us,
We laugh as loud as he roars!

KYUNG
(Korean—respect)
Really likes snack time,
Juice and grapes are favorites she ranks.
But before taking one bite,
Respectfully she gives thanks.

LARS
(Danish – crowned with laurels)
Signals 'go' with a crown
To be placed on the winner's head.
The runner who finishes first
Reaps laurels of yellow and red.

M

MAVERICK
(American – independent)
Paints beautiful horses.
Better than any you'll see.
He's an artist who's amazing,
And independent as can be!

NESSA
(Greek - butterfly)
Flits from here to there
Spreading her wings out far,
A butterfly of bright colors,
Glowing like the morning star!

OREB
(Israeli - raven)
Roosts on the jungle gym
Watching the children below,
Like a raven in the treetops,
Getting ready to swoop down low.

PILAR
(Mexican – column)
Builds with lots of blocks,
Making tall columns so high.
When adding roofs and chimneys.
His work nearly touches the sky!

QUINN
(Irish – wisdom, counsel)
Sees there is trouble
With two little girls nearby.
Quickly she offers wise counsel,
"Forgive and forget, won't you try?"

RAJESH
(Indian – king)
Wears a fine red robe,
And speaks from his royal seat.
As king of the class today,
His message for fun can't be beat!

SOMMER
(German – summer)
Climbs on a strong tree branch
And longs for bright, sunny days.
While her friends play games below,
She dreams of the ocean's blue waves.

TYESHA
(African - American – alive and well)
Missed school last week.
She had the sniffles and flu.
So glad she's returned today,
Now well and as good as new!

UTA
(Japanese – song)
Sings so beautifully
As she strums on her guitar,
Songs we've never heard before,
From a distant land so far.

VANDER
(Swedish – strong fighter)
Flexes his muscles
To show how strong he can be,
But he never hits or punches
'Cause he wouldn't hurt a flea!

WILLOW
(English – graceful)
Sways so gracefully
To a sweet-sounding melody.
As some friends sit beside her,
Others dance along merrily.

XALVADOR
(Spanish – savior)
The good savior,
Hurries to help those in need.
He tends to their bumps and bruises,
As a doctor, doing kind deeds.

YAHOLO
(Native-American – he who yells)
Yells loudly for us
To see what creatures he's found.
A wiggly worm, a slimy snail,
He's spied while digging the ground.

ZOYA
(Slavic – dawn)
Rises like the dawn,
Bringing happiness to our day.
She is kind, helpful and sweet,
In a gentle and giving way.

Now that you've met all of us,
Preschool friends from A to Z
Together we can change the world
Living in peace and harmony!

ABOUT THE AUTHOR

During her professional career, Flo Barnett was a preschool administrator and day-care provider. She also taught kindergarten and elementary school for many years.

Now retired, Flo writes hilarious tales for, and sometimes based on the real-life antics of her seven grandchildren whom she lovingly refers to as 'Grammy's Gang.'

Ms. Barnett has also written a series entitled, 'When We Were Kids.' The books are set in the Fifties and deal with issues such as peer pressure, bullying, abuse, and personal loss. Since today's children face the same problems as did their parents and grandparents, this series is geared for ages 9-99.

Currently Flo is working on a third series, 'Together In Peace And Harmony,' hoping to encourage youngsters to embrace diversity rather than fear it. She believes that the only way to attain peace in the world is to begin by teaching children at the preschool level to interact positively with others from various ethnic and cultural backgrounds.
Flo lives near Pittsburgh, Pennsylvania, with her hubby, Barry, and dog, Shadow.

FLO BARNETT'S SERIES INCLUDE:

TOGETHER IN PEACE AND HARMONY
>>*Preschool Friends A-Z Around The World, Book 1*

WHEN WE WERE KIDS
>>*Playing Hooky, Book 1*
>>*Puppy Love, Book 2*
>>*Pimples And Periods, Book 3*
>>*Promises, Book 4*

GRAMMY'S GANG
>>*No Way To Haircut Day! Book 1*
>>*Dirty Face Liam, Book 2*
>>*Calling All Grammies, Book 3*
>>*There's A Baby In Mommy's Belly! Book 4*
>>*Sweet, Sweet, Sweet Barefeet! Book 5*
>>*When Grammy Goes Away, Book 6*
>>*Yo! Baby, Go! Go, Baby! Book 7*

For more information, please contact Flo at:
www.amazon.com/flobarnett
www.grammysgangbooks.blogspot.com
Twitter: FloBarnett@FloBarnett1

For information about James Ambrous visit:
JamesAmbrous.com
James@JamesAmbrous.com

Printed in Great Britain
by Amazon